Ragtime Pia s

44 Authentic Rags

Cover Painting by Mary Woodin - London, England

ISBN 0-634-09632-X

7777 W. BLUEMOUND RD. P.O. BOX 13819 MILWAUKEE, WI 53213

In Australia Contact:
Hal Leonard Australia Pty. Ltd.
4 Lentara Court
Cheltenham, Victoria, 3192 Australia
Email: ausadmin@halleonard.com

Visit Hal Leonard Online at
www.halleonard.com

CONTENTS

AMERICAN BEAUTY

By JOSEPH LAMB

L.H.
1
2
mf

f dim.
fz mp
cresc.

1
2
8
f
mf
Ped.
*

ANTOINETTE

By SCOTT JOPLIN

Tempo di Marcia

mf

mf

f

mf

mf

1
2
f
f
Ped.
*
Ped.
*
Ped.
*
1
2

TRIO.
p
p
mf
R.H.
sempre f
R.H.

mp
f
ff

A BLACK SMOKE

By CHARLES L. JOHNSON

p
ff
p
ff
p
ff

3

THE CASCADES

By SCOTT JOPLIN

r.h.
l.h.
mf
1.
2.

p – f
Ped.
p – f
1.
2.
Fine.

CHAMPAGNE RAG

By JOSEPH LAMB

ff sempre marcato.
mf

TRIO.
mp legato!
f

f
8
ff
ffz ff
1
2

DILL PICKLES

By CHARLES JOHNSON

1.
2.
ff

mf
mf
TRIO.
f
p
f

f
p
ff
1.
2.
ff

DIMPLES

By L.E. COLBURN

1.
2.
ff
ffz

p
f
p
f
p
f
1.
2.
p-ff

p
f
p
f
p
f
ffz

THE EASY WINNERS

By SCOTT JOPLIN

1.
2.
1.
2.

1.
2.
1.
2.

ENCORE RAG

By TAD FISCHER

1
2

3
3
3
1
2
8
8

HARLEM RAG

By TOM TURPIN

ff
ff

mf

THE ENTERTAINER

By SCOTT JOPLIN

1.
2.
Repeat 8va.
f
p
p
1.
8
2.

p
f
p
f
p
f
f

1.
2.
fz
f
1.
2.

THE FASCINATOR

By JAMES SCOTT

f
repeat 8va.

FELICITY RAG

By SCOTT JOPLIN

1
2
f
1
2

p
1
2

1
2

FIG LEAF RAG

By SCOTT JOPLIN

f
1
2
f
8
1
2

mf
mf
f
p legato
8
p

mf
1
2
mf
mp
1
2
Fine.

GLADIOLUS RAG

By SCOTT JOPLIN

f
mf
f
1
2

mf
R. H.
L. H.
R. H.
L. H.
R. H.
L. H.
mp
Ped.

Ped.
mf
sostenuto sempre
f legato

GRACE AND BEAUTY

By JAMES SCOTT

f—mp
f
1.
f
2.
8
f

ff
f
l.h.
TRIO.
ff
sfz
p-f
8

8
1.
2.
mf-f
8
8
p
8
8

INVITATION RAG

By LES C. COPELAND

1
2
mf

f
fz

HILARITY RAG

By JAMES SCOTT

Not fast.

8

mf

8

8

1

2

8
8
1
2
p - mf
8

1
2
mf
8
1
2

KISMET RAG

By SCOTT JOPLIN
and SCOTT HAYDEN

1
2
1
2

KITTEN ON THE KEYS

By ZEZ CONFREY

D♭
p dolce
A♭7
E♭m
A♭7
B♭m
E♭
A♭7
D♭
A♭7
E♭m6
B7
E
B7
D♭
A♭7
1
A♭7
D♭
2
D♭
Am
G
Gm
F
Fm
E♭
E♭m
D♭
Cm
B♭
D♭m
C
B°
C
Fm
F

G7 Am Gm6 G7 C7 F G9
C F G7 Am Gm6
G7 C7 F C7 F
TRIO F E♭m6 F E♭m6 F B♭6 G♯o F
ff
Dm F♯o Gm Dm F♯ Gm Dm B♭m C7
mf
F7 B♭ A7

B♭
Dm F♯o
8
Gm Dm
F♯o Gm Dm
B♭m F7
A♭o
C7
F7
A♭
F7
Dm F♯o
8
Gm Dm
F♯o Gm Dm
B♭m C7
F7
D
D7
G7 C7 G Dm
Co Em G
Am Co Em
Am
Co C
F7
B♭
F7 B♭

MAGNETIC RAG

By SCOTT JOPLIN

mf
f
mf
f
1
2

mf
cresc.
f
mf
f
mf
cresc.
f
1
2

Tempo l'istesso
mf
mf cresc. poco a poco
ff
mf
mf
f
f

f sempre
1
2
r.h.
l.h.
Fine

MAPLE LEAF RAG

By SCOTT JOPLIN

f stacc.
1.
2.
f
p
r. h.
l. h.
r. h.
l. h.
mf

TRIO.
1.
2.
1.
2.

MEMPHIS BLUES

Words and Music by
W.C. HANDY

ff
ff
8va
loco
1.
2.

mp
legato
f
ff
legato

PEACHES AND CREAM

By PERCY WENRICH

TRIO.

PLEASANT MOMENTS

By SCOTT JOPLIN

mf
mf
f
1
2
mf

f
p cantabile
mp
1
2

mf
f
ff
poco
accel
Fine.

QUALITY RAG

By JAMES SCOTT

1.
8
3
2.
mf - f
8
8
8
1.
2.
8
3

8
3
8
8
p
8
8

8
1.
2.
8
ff
8
f
8
8
8
8
8

RAG TIME CHIMES

By PERCY WENRICH

1.
2.
f
p
f
p
f
p
f
p
1.
2.

p
p - f
L.H.

1.
2.

RAGTIME NIGHTINGALE

By JOSEPH LAMB

L. H.
1
2
mp

mp
fz

R. H.
L. H.
mf
f
ff
fz

RAGTIME ORIOLE

By JAMES SCOTT

L.H.
L.H.
R.H.
R.H. L.H.
1
2
8
f
8
1
2

FINE.
TRIO.

D.C. 𝄋 to Fine.

SEARCHLIGHT RAG

By SCOTT JOPLIN

f legato
ff
f
1.
2.

mf
mf
f
mp legato
f

mp
1.
2.
f
f
mp legato
f
mp
1.
2.
f

SENSATION

By JOSEPH LAMB

mf - ff
cresc.
f stac.
fz

Trio.
f-ff
cresc.
fz
ff marc.
cresc.
mf
ff
fz
8

THE THRILLER RAG

By MAY AUFDERHEIDE

p-mf
1
2
ff

ff
ff

SOMETHING DOING

By SCOTT JOPLIN
and SCOTT HAYDEN

1
2
1
2

f
p

f
1
2
Fine.

ST. LOUIS BLUES

Words and Music by
W.C. HANDY

1
2
f
p
8
8
loco
3

f
p
8
loco
8
3
ff
Plaintive
p
l. h.
l. h.
f
rit.
a tempo

f
ff
p
sfz
l. h.
rit.
f
Brightly
a tempo
rit.

ST. LOUIS TICKLE

By BARNEY and SEYMORE

ff
p
1
2
mf
1
2

f
f
1
2
ff
p

ff
p
ff
ff

SUGAR CANE

By SCOTT JOPLIN

2
f
mp
1
2

mf
mp

mf
mp
Fine.

SWEET PICKLES

By GEORGE E. FLORENCE

ff
1
2
1
2

mf
f
mf
ff

1
2
ff

THE TEMPTATION RAG

By HENRY LODGE

f
mf stacc.
f
f

A TENNESSEE TANTALIZER

By CHARLES HUNTER

THAT SCANDALOUS RAG

By EDWIN F. KEMDALL

mf
cresc.
f
p

p
p
TRIO
p

mf
Fine
B.Dr.
mf
f
ff
ff
Trio D.C. al Fine

THAT TEASIN' RAG

By JOE JORDAN

mp–f
1
2

Trio.
cresc.
mp - f

1
2
f
fz
D. C.

TOO MUCH MUSTARD

By CECIL MACKLIN

f
3
p
3
p
f

Trio.
mf
p
mf
f
mf
1
f
2
f
p
3
3
f

mf
f
p
f
Fine.

TWELFTH STREET RAG

By EUDAY L. BOWMAN

mf

(♭)

mf
8va

f
mf

sfz

WILD CHERRIES RAG

By TED SNYDER

f
f
1
2
f
mf
fz

Trio
p
f
p
f
f

8
8
cresc
8va. ad lib.
ff
3
3
f
3
3
f
loco
1
2
8
fz

YOUR FAVORITE MUSIC

ARRANGED FOR PIANO SOLO

Broadway – 20 Piano Solos

Play rich piano solo arrangements of 20 Broadway favorites! Includes: All I Ask of You • And All That Jazz • Can You Feel the Love Tonight • Edelweiss • The Impossible Deam • Memory • On My Own • Put On a Happy Face • Seasons of Love • Some Enchanted Evening • Summer Nights • Tomorrow • Unexpected Song • and more!

00311028 .... $12.95

Classic Broadway Solos

16 beautifully arranged Broadway standards including: I Could Have Danced All Night • If Ever I Would Leave You • The Impossible Dream • Memory • Smoke Gets in Your Eyes • You'll Never Walk Alone • and more.

00294002 .... $12.95

Classical Themes from the Movies

Over 31 familiar and favorite themes, including: Also Sprach Zarathustra • Ave Maria • Canon in D • Habanera • Overture to *The Marriage of Figaro* • and more.

00221010 .... $9.95

Definitive Classical Collection

129 selections. Includes music by Johann Sebastian Bach, Ludwig van Beethoven, Johannes Brahms, Frederic Chopin, Claude Debussy, George Frideric Handel, Felix Mendelssohn, Johann Pachelbel, Franz Schubert, Pyotr Tchaikovsky, Richard Wagner, and many more!

00310772 .... $29.95

Jazz Standards

15 all-time favorite songs, including: All The Things You Are • Bluesette • I'll Remember April • Mood Indigo • Satin Doll • and more.

00292055 .... $12.95

Billy Joel Easy Classics

This unique collection includes 17 of his best songs: Honesty • It's Still Rock and Roll to Me • The Longest Time • Movin' Out (Anthony's Song) • My Life • Piano Man • Roberta • She's Got a Way • Uptown Girl • more.

00306202 .... $12.95

Lennon & McCartney Piano Solos

22 beautiful arrangements, including: Eleanor Rigby • The Fool on the Hill • Here, There and Everywhere • Lady Madonna • Let It Be • Yesterday • and more.

00294023 .... $14.95

Andrew Lloyd Webber

14 pieces, including: All I Ask of You • Don't Cry for Me Argentina • Memory • The Music of the Night • Phantom of the Opera • Pie Jesu • and more.

00292001 .... $14.95

Love & Wedding Piano Solos

26 contemporary and classic wedding favorites, including: All I Ask of You • Ave Maria • Endless Love • Through the Years • Vision of Love • Sunrise, Sunset • Don't Know Much • Unchained Melody • and more.

00311507 .... $12.95

Memorable Jazz Standards

24 elegant favorites: Autumn in New York • Autumn Leaves • Body and Soul • How Deep Is the Ocean • Isn't It Romantic? • It Might as Well Be Spring • My Funny Valentine • Satin Doll • Stella by Starlight • The Very Thought of You • When I Fall in Love • more.

00310719 .... $12.95

Movie Piano Solos

20 rich arrangements, including: The Exodus Song • The Firm Main Title • The Godfather (Love Theme) • Moon River • Raider's March • Theme From Schindler's List • When I Fall in Love • A Whole New World • and more.

00311675 .... $10.95

Elvis Presley Pianos Solos

A great collection of over 15 of The King's best, including: Are You Lonesome Tonight? • Don't Be Cruel • It's Now or Never • Love Me Tender • All Shook Up • and more.

00292002 .... $9.95

Sacred Inspirations

arr. Phillip Keveren

11 songs, featuring: How Majestic Is Your Name • Great Is the Lord • Amazing Grace • Friends • Via Dolorosa • In the Name of the Lord • and more.

00292057 .... $9.95

Shout to the Lord

Moving arrangements of 14 praise favorites as interpreted by Phillip Keveren: As the Deer • El Shaddai • How Beautiful • How Majestic Is Your Name • More Precious Than Silver • Oh Lord, You're Beautiful • Shine, Jesus, Shine • Shout to the Lord • and more.

00310699 .... $12.95

Showcase for Piano

Intermediate to advanced arrangements of 18 popular songs: Bali Ha'i • Bewitched • I Can't Get Started with You • I Could Write a Book • I'll Be Seeing You • My Funny Valentine • September Song • Where or When • You'll Never Walk Alone • and more.

00310664 .... $8.95

TV Themes

33 classic themes, including: Addams Family • Alfred Hitchcock Presents • The Brady Bunch • (Meet) The Flintstones • Home Improvement • Mister Ed • Northern Exposure • This Is It (Bugs Bunny Theme) • Twin Peaks • and more.

00292030 .... $10.95